writer fuel

Be Inspired to Start and Finish Your Story

Cassie Newell

writer fuel

WRITER FUEL: Be Inspired to Start and Finish Your Story

Copyright © 2022 Cassie Newell

Publisher: Sassy Press (First published October 2022)

Cover Designer: Booklytical Designs

Internal Format Art: Cassie Newell

All rights reserved. No part of this this publication may be reproduced, stored in any retrieval system, copied in any form or by any means, electronic, mechanical, photocopying, recording or otherwise transmitted, without permission of the copyright owner. Except for a reviewer who may quote brief passages in a review.

Print ISBN: 978-0-9976836-9-1

Hardback ISBN: 978-1-956049-02-2

ebook ISBN: 978-1-956049-00-8

www.sassywritingcoach.com

All rights reserved

table of contents

The Reader Intro	1
1. In the Beginning	7
2. Name It before You Start It	13
3. Start before You Are Ready	21
4. Do the Work and Play	31
5. Establishing WHY	45
6. Disconnection and Creativity	57
7. Quitting vs. a Sticking Tactic vs. a Strategy	69
8. Zigging and Zagging	77
9. The Beauty of Finished	89
10. A Sassy Mindset	97
Mindset Review	103
Author's Note	105
Bibliography	107
Endnotes	109
About the Author	111
Acknowledgments	113
Other Titles by Cassie Newell	115

To you, the writer, who fearlessly crafts words and worlds onto a blank page. This is for you.

the reader intro

YOUR PURCHASE of this book reveals some important details about you—you have a spark of an idea, and the desire to write your story down to share it with others—and that these pieces *mean* something to you. It also tells me that because these details are important, you likely fall into one of the following thought patterns:

1. You've got a spark and desire and want to keep them,
2. You want the spark and desire to persist while you finish your project no matter what stage it is in,
3. You've lost your spark and desire, and you're in the pit of despair, needing to be pulled out.

You could be at the very beginning of your writing journey, aiming to maximize all aspects and energy so you can finish your story without the disruptions of writer's block or other tales of doom you've heard around forums or on social media. It could be you are at the midway point right now—and you haven't touched your manuscript in *forever*. Or you may have already read this book, and you're coming back to it to be inspired and recall a few steps to get you back on track.

Motivation is like a campfire. You light the flame, but if you don't tend to it over time, it burns out.

The point of this book is to help you tend to your individual writer fire and to give you the permission to be inspired and motivated. This book is more than a match, it's fuel to keep your flame burning constant. The goal is not to light the fire and watch it burn down and out; the goal is for you to have the fuel to burn until you reach the destination. Allow this book to be **your** personal motivational manifesto for writing. I'll be your guide, but the direction and the vehicle are up to *you*. This is your motivation we are tapping into, and the first thing to do is:

WRITER FUEL

What could I possibly be talking about? First, the permission is for buying this book and reading it. But I'm really referring to the deeper self-permission that allows you to truly absorb the content, and when I ask questions, to not only think on them, but write your thoughts out, dare I say, **in this book**.

If marking up this book or e-book will cause you great pain, then I begrudgingly say fine, don't do it. But do write somewhere when prompted or whenever you're inspired. You can use a journal or a notebook of your choice, like a glitter one that begs to be used, or one where it has thick paper that you can use your favorite fountain pen. Choose a notebook or journal that is all *you*! I've also pulled together a free companion PDF (located at www.sassywritingcoach.com/extrafuel) for you, dear reader, should you prefer something that is collated from this book. The reason for writing is so you can come back to your answers, recall them, evolve, and change them as you grow, because your own motivation is the fuel for the fire.

Don't knock the permission, and do not skip this step because granting permission is the most freeing start. Trust me, I know this because I had to give it to myself. I have all kinds of responsibilities like everyone else, but I'm also chasing this dream while working a full-time demanding career, being a wife, and raising two fabulous daughters. I get pulled in different directions all the time, but I realized showing my daughters how to go after what they want, instead of only speaking to it, was much more powerful. So, lean into who you are and what responsibilities you have and allow yourself the permission to pursue this goal, because actions do speak louder than words.

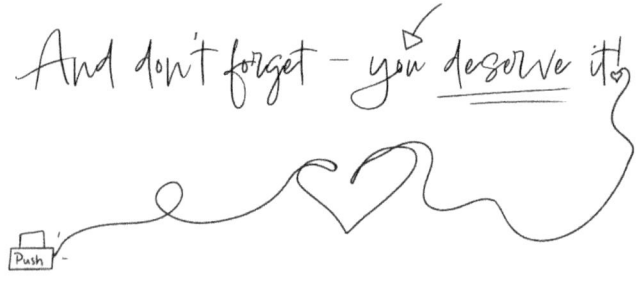

Be honest with yourself—this book will evolve as you evolve, so remember what I said above. Come back to it when you need the motivation and inspiration to fuel your fire. Let's get started, my friend, and uncover why I wrote this book and why you needed this book. But first, claim your permission to do so, and let's begin by you writing it down. Make that claim and stake it.

WRITER FUEL

Permission Slip

Name: _____ Date: _____

in the beginning

SOME SAY STARTING IS the hardest part of writing. I disagree. Starts are easy, middles and endings are hard.

To me, starts and discoveries are the best. They are all about the exciting momentum that builds up and propels action forward. It's like when you meet someone for the first time and you're smitten. Then, as you're around them more, the attraction builds deeper, and it becomes passion. You're driven to this person, but beyond passion, what remains is a relationship, something deeper. The same progression happens with writing your novel, your memoir, your collection of short stories.

So, who am I to write a book about motivation?

I am an author, a writing coach, a graphic designer, a people manager, a team leader, a project manager, a mentor, a wife, and a mother. Now that we've got all the titles and the roles out of the way, let's get down to brass tacks.

I am not a full-time author. I manage a professional career outside of writing books and coaching authors. In 2016, I decided that was the year I was going to finish my first fiction book for publication. I hired my first writing coach, and it was glorious. My first book was completed and published within six months. I submitted my book for review in the 2016 New Apple Awards. Why? Because I was on a high of my achievement and figured, why not?

When I got my email that I had won an award, I thought it was spam. Guess what, it wasn't! Needless to say, my first experience was surreal. It should have set me up in theory to keep going, right? Remember that high I spoke about? Well, nine months later, in 2017, I was in the pit of despair, completely unmotivated and uninspired on the promising, successful road that I had built for myself.

Cry me a river, right?

I was in writing paralysis. I couldn't seem to get it together. Hard on the heels of the award-winner high, in waltzed shiny new object syndrome, clad as another story idea, which began summoning me to write it instead of continuing the series of my current, successfully published book. This new story took over; I was knee-deep into outlining and mapping the entire concept with hired coaches. I was falling in love with the process—this new story idea, the characters, the potential. Essentially, I was inspired to write a full novel again. Then, in 2018 I attended a writing conference where I was networking and got even more motivated. When I wasn't chatting with someone and attending the conference, I was writing in my hotel room. It was a creative, passionate pull, and it was electric!

What I wasn't inspired to do was to look back at my first book that had been planned as a three-book series. I asked the opinions of the coaches I had worked with and discussed it with my new coach and editor. The consensus was that I should complete what I had started, since the first book was published and had a readership. The new idea wasn't going anywhere; it could wait in the wings. I decided to follow through and get more practice under my belt. To finish my series before I tackled the shiny object; the book I was dying to write and publish.

I put my experience as a leader and manager to use, called on my ability to mentor and coach, and invoked my ability to pivot (let's face it, as adults and especially parents, we know how to pivot, whether successfully or not). There were several stumbles along the way, including a full burnout, and some major insights and successes. That first series is complete and published, along with a related novella. Since 2019, I've been coaching clients and authors, motivating and propelling them toward their writing goals.

So, let's say I know a little something about motivation and what drives people. I also understand that surface level responses and rationale will break apart and not hold you afloat in rough waters.

> *Sheer determination toward a goal is short-term thinking.*

This book is <u>not</u> an instruction on how to tell a story, or the process of crafting a story and developing characters. This book is all about you—the writer, the person who has a goal to finish a story, a novel, your book. It could be your first novel in your career, it could be your twentieth; heck, it could even be your planned last hurrah in a series that you've been dragging your feet on. The goal of this book is to provide you with some tools for diving deep into your writer's fuel. And hopefully along the way, a few aha moments, and something that really resonates within you to keep you going up to writing 'The End.'

Remember: You have permission to write in this book.
Highlight, make notes. Even, dare I say, dog ear the pages - gasp!
Make this your book above all else, it needs to be meaningful for you.

This is a book that I needed in 2016 when I started, and something I should have re-read in 2017. So, without further ado and with pomp and circumstance, let's dive in.

name it before you start it

"Ideas in secret die. They need light and air or they starve to death." – Seth Godin. [1]

WOULD it surprise you to learn how many different things can inspire someone to start a story? There are some common sources of inspiration, such as life changes, new experiences, and even just sitting down with a blank page or computer screen before you, poised for the first word and sentence. These moments in time are invigorating and motivational, marking the start of something special.

It's easy to think the start is in drafting, meaning the words and sentences that shape your story in a manuscript format. But at the end of the day, a story is only as good as its spark, i.e., the idea. That initial inspiration is what drives the entire story, so it's important to understand where it comes from. Identifying your spark can help you stay focused on what's important, and it can also give you a much-needed dose of motivation to draw on if you hit a rough patch along the way. Don't get bogged down in the drafting yet—that's next.

Let's begin with that spark; the piece that is calling to you to craft a story.

It might be a scene, a character, or a fascinating bit of history that you stumbled upon. You must name it, and I'm not referring to a novel title. Give whatever ignited that frisson of excitement a specific label that has significance to you. When you label it, you'll have an even better chance of understanding, recalling, and reaching for that inspirational spark when you need it.

Forget the censoring, too. If the moment gave you flashbacks to 1992 when the guy you were interested in was holding off on kissing

you to show you were more to him than a causal fling, so instead you initiate the first kiss—because honestly, who waits after a couple dates? You might label that spark after him, for example, to connect to that feeling or that moment. Name and label it for **you**—it's your fire that you're lighting.

Actions cause reactions

When I name my inspiration and put it out there, it becomes tangible. It's no longer something that is ruminating in my mind without shape. Take the action of naming as your beginning. If you are hesitant in putting a label to a spark, it could be that when you do, it becomes an actionable task. This is just the point; when the spark is something you'd like to try on, think of it as trying on clothes at a shop; there is no commitment until you buy.

The singular beginning is motivation, like window shopping before walking into the store. Even if you walk into a store not knowing exactly what you want, there was a spark that guided you into the store, if we stay with this analogy. You must label your spark. And it's perfectly fine for the spark to not be a fully formed thing yet.

But Cassie, I'm confused, I have no idea what you mean!

OK, since you absolutely cannot skip this all-important initial step, I'll give you an example from my inspiration arsenal to illustrate this concept. My fiction work-in-progress at the time of writing this book is about monsters that are both literal and figurative— stuff that scares and has scared me, especially when I was a teen —and how to tell the difference between them. I love playing with ideas and notions of what is expected versus the reality of how things really are. This is my spark and the label I chose was a character from a book that prompted my spark. It's not super defined on who, what, and when, but that is exactly the point. It's all mine to mold later. Remember, you are searching for the initial spark.

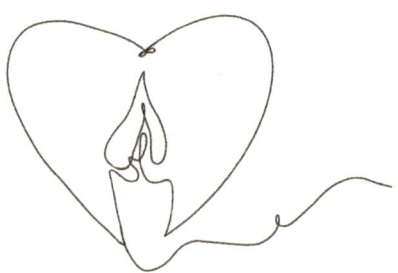

You don't have to know everything on page one. That is the BIGGEST mistake new writers make, and I've seen a few experienced ones make it too because they put too much pressure on themselves to know more than they are really able to know at this stage.

The naming is an essential part of the process, take the time you need to give the spark some definition. Ask yourself why this idea is something you are drawn to. It can be absolutely anything. It only needs to make sense to you. Take a moment to label your spark and write it down so that it's meaningful for **you**.

Don't let your spark starve.
What if I have no spark?

For those of you without a spark yet, this is for you. Perhaps you turned to this book to find a new idea to build a story on.

But where do you go to find the basis for a story?

For some people, music is a great source of inspiration. Listening to the right song at the right time can completely change your mood and get those creative juices flowing. If you're feeling stuck, try putting on your favorite album and notice what lyrics or melodies jump out at you. The effects music has on us at energetic and vibrational levels can be the perfect igniter of creativity.

Another common source of story generation is nature. There's something about being surrounded by the beauty of the natural world that can make even the most mundane things seem interesting and worth writing about. If you're struggling to come up with ideas, take a walk outside and see what catches your eye.

Sometimes, all it takes is a writing prompt or two to get the wheels turning. Whether it's coming up with an interesting character or situation, or just writing a few sentences to start things off, prompts can be a great way to jump-start your creativity. If you're feeling uninspired, try searching writing prompts online or in print and see if any of them trigger ideas for your spark.

Two final channels of inspiration that often work for me are reading or watching shows on my television, computer, or at the theater. I love thinking about how I would have done a concept differently or what would happen if a character's choice went in another direction. Fan fiction is a powerful thing for practicing and inspiring your storyteller skills. It can be fun mixing and matching character types and story plots. Unicorn cowboys, anyone? Consuming stories in one format or another is a little springboard to prompt the inspiration station of your brain.

The key to knowing if your idea is truly the ignition for the spark is pressure testing its long-term excitement for you for completing a full story: beginning, middle, and end. Remember that one shirt, or outfit you had to have that still hangs in your closet, but you've only worn once? Yeah, you know what I'm talking about. Make sure this is an outfit you find joy in wearing most days. In the next chapter, I talk more on how to pressure test, which is starting to write down more about your spark in a story format. It takes your initial idea and molds it into a premise.

Not all ideas are meant for the long haul and that's OK. Some will spur on new thought trains and journeys to follow at another time. Others may end up as story threads you weave in as you draft and revise. Having a file of ideas ready to be explored is something many writers do.

start before you are ready

"You miss 100% of the shots you don't take." – *Wayne Gretzky*[1]

HOW MANY TIMES have you started something? Remember when I said, 'starting is the best?'

I'm one of those people who will jump off the springboard into the pool, but if I have to climb a ladder on a high dive and saunter out—it gives me too much time to think. I don't want to go down the way I came. It's partly my bravado, but I'd rather move forward and jump than retreat.

What holds some back is the doubt and the need for preparation. There exists in the writing world a preconceived notion that you must know *everything* before you start. The everything can be broken down into two parts: your story idea and the craft of writing. Both, frankly, are rabbit holes.

The need to know everything can become an excuse and a crutch for not beginning to write (I would never say that to a new surgeon, they need to know what they are doing before that first cut). It's not as if you don't know how to write. You've been writing your whole life since you were in primary school. I will take it for granted that you know how to put words onto paper or a screen in the language of your choice.

The obstacles to beginning are, instead, fear and your definition of success. Like me, you're thinking because you're climbing that ladder to the high dive. You don't need to start by diving into the pool. Starting is as simple as dipping your toe in the water or taking the stairs into the shallow end. If your personality is to jump —then jump, I won't fault you for it. Just be prepared; that cool water can be jarring.

Set apart the idea that you need to know everything first—just begin.

The goal and purpose for writing a story are different for everyone. For some, the goal might be getting a book published. For others, it might simply be enjoying the process and sharing their work with friends. But if you don't start, you'll never finish, and that is the point.

There is a ton of advice out there telling you to dive in regarding how to start your draft:

- Write a synopsis, create an outline, and write the story following that outline.
- Be prepared for revisions, start with your first three chapters, and write 2000 words per chapter.
- Do all your character profiles, write your last chapter first.
- If you're a discovery writer (slang term - pantser), here's the way, or too bad, you need to be a plotter or vice versa.

The thing is, specifically if this is your first book, your first story—**you are a blank page**. You don't know yet what areas you need to work on, what you prefer, or how one way is better for you or your story than another. This is a gift!

Don't get bogged down in labeling yourself on how you write and what that process is quite yet. Push all of that away, because reading that list above is daunting; don't let it frustrate you.

For those of you who are on your second, fifth, or tenth book—lean into the start and the refreshing blank page; reset your beginning. Embrace the excitement!

"Don't be intimidated by what you don't know. That can be your greatest strength and ensure that you do things differently from everyone else." – Sara Blakely[2]

The key to creativity is to start. If inherently you know yourself and you are a planner—then plan. That is you starting.

Suppose you know you perform best by having all the knowledge at the outset. Then consume all the books on writing craft beforehand, and then consume stories in your genre—that is you starting.

For me, I'm a visual person and I dabble with mood boards and quick ideas of character, plot, and emotion—this is me starting.

This is creativity. There is no right or wrong way.

The prior point acknowledged that the definition of starting varies from person to person. For the purposes of this book, starting is discovering what you are going to write, what the story is, the theme(s) or situation that you want to explore. Is it a specific character or plot point that has you excited? It doesn't have to be complicated. Like naming it, here you are digging deeper into the outcome you want to achieve by first discovering it. For some, this may be something intuitive to you, and for others, you may have to uncover it.

Did you know as a writer you first are an adventurer?

There may only be a finite number of plots to a story, but you, my friend, are the unique special sauce to its outcome. Adventure beyond what you think you know and challenge yourself in order to receive the breadth and depth to grow in your creativity. Sometimes we accept what we learn at a surface level, and, in many cases, that is fine and what is needed. I'm challenging you when it comes to a creative pursuit. There is a sense of satisfaction in a deeper-rooted discovery.

I'm an artist at heart and I look at stories in the same vein of creativity. However, my writing clients have taught me that some people embrace their artistic side while others try to put it in a box. Until you begin revising and editing, give yourself permission to color outside the lines, as an adventurer. Give yourself permission to find your own terms and boundaries, not someone else's. I learned at an early age that creativity is in the eye of the beholder, and your creativity is specifically yours, along with your continually developing process.

My uncle Doug is an artist as well. I admired him while growing up because I was a budding artist. He was daring with his artwork, and it was colorful. He captured his subjects so clearly, like a photograph. During one visit to his house, I was rummaging through his garage and found a canvas covered with splashes of paint, but no recognizable subject. It was abstract, and it was all new to me. When he found me in the garage, I asked what it was, because a toddler, or literally anyone, could create that. His face didn't display any disappointment in what surely was a little stab to the heart. Instead, his simple reply to me was, "Anyone didn't do it, I did it." Can I tell you how wide the world opened for me in that simple response? I was no longer *envious* of my uncle's art and talent. I understood the value of appreciating not only his ability, but my unique talent as well. Appreciation often inspires creativity.

Later, in high school, I was considered one of the top students in the art department with another student, Mike. He had a distinctive style and talent from me. I appreciated it more than anything else—he unwittingly pushed me to be better and to try new things. Let your favorite stories and authors push you to be better. Like a favorite book or story that you cherish, what is it that you want to integrate into your own craft?

Explore this and dissect why you like certain authors or other story tellers, such as directors; dive into what you enjoy and how you want to emulate that in your work. Is it an idea? A style? Try not to be comparative, do this in the spirit of understanding and personal growth.

My art was appreciated on its own merit and had I not taken in what my uncle said to me, I might not have pursued practicing more and learning more, finding my own way and style. In writing, this is what many call your voice, because it's uniquely you.

I tell you this story because there will be times you will compare your stories to others. You will look at what other authors are doing, and either be fueled or completely gassed and defeated by their output. The point is you are not part of those equations of who and what you are comparing yourself to.

You are the special sauce to your stories, your writing, and your creative output.

No one has what you have, and that is everything.

You are the person for the story you want to write.

If there is something I could go back in time and tell my younger self, it would be to start writing sooner. I didn't write my first book until I was close to forty years old. I wish I had started sooner, but the fact of the matter was, I didn't know how or where to start—I was a completely blank page in knowing how to write a book. When I finally decided to sit down and do it, I aimed to complete it in six months, knowing little about the process and having only a spark and what I liked to read as motivation. The key for me was starting with a coach for accountability and not overthinking each move along the way. The uninformed timeline I gave myself didn't allow me to overthink very much.

You will never feel 100% ready to do anything because there is always something else you can learn or another way to accomplish things. But if you don't start, you

can never move forward.

"Trying is winning in the moment." – Dan Waldschmidt[3]

Part of book coaching is helping people take that first step in their stories. As a coach myself, writers come to me with ideas but are afraid to start because they don't know everything about the topic or how to execute it perfectly. I tell them all the same thing—start now and we will figure it out as you go. Execution comes later; put a pin on that topic for after edits.

This book is all about finding and maintaining the motivation to finish your first, roughest draft. You will make mistakes, but that is part of the journey, and it is how you will learn and become better at what you do. It's practice. Writing takes practice, and perfection is the devil in finishing and publication. Remove that word "perfection" and the thought from your mind. And don't worry about being perfect, because there is no such thing.

So, ready, set—go, spark the starting into a flame.

Remember, there is no right or wrong.

Say it with me, there is no such thing as perfection.

do the work and play

YOU'VE JUST STARTED your story, and it feels like you're playing with something completely abstract, an initial idea, or a story that's quite clear in your mind.

This is the fun, this is the excitement, right? I hope it is for you like it is for me; however, for some, I know it is the worst part. So, let's talk about that because embarking on this adventure should be play—it should be fun.

Writing a story is a creative pursuit, and it isn't only for someone who defines themself as a creative. It's not an exclusive activity. Yes, **anyone** can do it, and I thoroughly believe this.

There is a line in the movie *Sweet Home Alabama* that says being southern is a state of mind.[1] I feel the same way about creativity.

Creativity is not something you do, it's your state of mind.

Have you ever watched a child do a craft at school in which they create something? The smile and joy on their face is pure abandon. They are on a mission and enjoying the process the entire way through. **The key to creativity is not intelligence, it's imagination**. And the key to imagination is play. This creative state is called **playful intelligence**[2] because it is acted out through purposeful playing and not recreation.

Playful intelligence is the ability to think creatively and enjoy the process of making something. This is essential for writers, as it allows you to experiment and explore different ideas without worrying about the outcome. Playful intelligence allows us to be in a mental flow state that fosters the opportunity to produce our best work.

When I'm drafting and find I'm struggling, often it's because I'm not geared to create and play—the writing has become work. The difference between work and play, for me, is the have-tos that accompany work. The push but not the anticipation of pushing forward. This is when the line of enjoyment is crossed, and I veer into struggle and frustration. When I recognize this, I take a mental break so that when I come back, my mindset is of play, especially when I'm writing fiction and specifically when I'm drafting. That sounds crazy simple, doesn't it? It can be.

Right about now, you may be rolling your eyes at the idea that achieving the creative mindset is simple.

It can't be that easy, Cassie!

Settle down, settle down. Allow me to share with you my three simple "S" story secrets for cultivating a playful intelligence mindset during the drafting process.

**3 Simple Story Secrets for Drafting
Sight - Speech - Sentiment**

SIGHT

The first "S" is Sight, meaning I don't type, or write a lot when I start a new story. There isn't much to see on the page in terms of words or full paragraphs. The sight component is strong for a lot of us, but it can also inhibit creativity while drafting. Sight is all about blocking criticism as a process while you're writing.

I took a writing class in which my instructor said I was editing too much when drafting. The problem with this is I was taking myself out of play. First, he asked me if I could type without looking at the keyboard, and yes, I am a skilled typist. Then he had me draft with my monitor blacked out (dim the light so you can't read it or turn it off entirely) so I couldn't see the words I was typing.

Sounds crazy, right?

I had all the excuses for not trying this idea ready in an instant. What if my fingers move off the keyboard slightly, and I have a bunch of nonsense or jumbled spelling mistakes? My instructor said something to the effect of, "So?" After picking up my self-assurance from the floor, I did as he suggested. I went on to finish my draft while in his class, without concentrating on the darkened monitor in front of me. He was right. It totally freed me. Try it for yourself.

Because I could not edit what I had just written, I got used to putting words down without second-guessing them. Before long, the monitor, whether on or off, induced my brain to move forward; corrections and edits were no longer a driving force. For me, it was about getting the draft down and the forward momentum of ideas, characters, plot, and chapters.

I like writing on paper or on my iPad. When writing, I do the same exercise and focus on the empty space I'm filling versus re-reading what I've written. Sometimes, I make notes on my smartphone. I vary it up quite a bit when drafting because, again, creativity is a mindset of freedom and vice versa, and I advise you not to put yourself in a box. Sometimes our eyes are critical and judgmental—turn them off for a bit and see if that helps the words flow.

SPEECH

The second "S" is Speech. Two of my favorite technology tools are voice notes and dictation. Speech is all about the inhibition of words during drafting. They allow me to get words down at any point in my day without worrying about how it sounds, which is not dissimilar to the darkened monitor of the Sight secret. Sure, I stumble and babble while recording, but my thought process keeps going, and I continue making forward progress with the story. It's like working through a scene or an idea with a collaborator, but you are your own collaborator. Sometimes I discover fabulous gems of ideas or phrases within this babble, but if I don't record or write it down, once it's off my lips, it's out of my ears and lost to me. Recording with voice notes or dictation software saves me from the frustration of a poor memory.

Hearing my own voice and working with an active train of thought does take getting used to, but I love it. My go-to application is Otter.ai[3] because it records voice memos and then transcribes them into a printed version I can cut and paste directly into my manuscript. If the transcription seems off, you can go back and listen to yourself to make the correction.

Dragon Anywhere[4] is another application I have used and liked because it's trainable to specific words and my unique voice and accent. For example, I had distinctive names for my young adult fantasy novel and although my character named Eoin is pronounced Owen, I didn't want to edit and correct it every time. I updated Dragon's dictionary with my series-relevant words, and between its artificial intelligence and a bit of 'training' it no longer spelled the name incorrectly. Sometimes I also use my computer's built-in dictation feature. They all help to get words onto the page and keep the drafting momentum rolling forward.

For dictation, there are so many options, I encourage you to give one or two a try. It is awkward at first, but once you get going, you'll find it really is beneficial in capturing thoughts in their original form.

SENTIMENT

The final "S" of my Simple Story Secrets is Sentiment, which is achieved through making a mood board. Sentiment is all about emotion.

A mood board is a visual collection of colors, characters, places, symbols, quotes—anything that embodies or defines a part of a story or a theme or an emotional response. It's a collection and representation that gives meaning to the story you are trying to create. I'm a visual person, so using images to record my thought patterns is instinctive and fun. It gets the wheel rolling for drafting and keeps my brain in play mode. You can do this on apps, on your computer, or on a poster board. The options are endless.

I prefer having most things in digital form, not only for ease of incorporation, but I am more efficient that way. I love using Pinterest and Milanote (both are applications on the internet). They are my go-tos. Typically, I have my mood boards open as I'm drafting, especially in the beginning, to refer to when necessary.

Another option for Sentiment is music. The beats, the words, the tone of a song invoke a similar mood for me. I create book scene playlists for myself. I have even pulled together songs specific to a character. In fact, I publish those playlists on Spotify for fans who enjoy my fiction books. It's a nice easter egg for my readers and fans, because after all, stories exist to evoke emotion and sentiment.

I encourage you to experiment, play, have fun! Discover what methods work for you to keep the words flowing and the creative flame burning.

The key to trying and experimenting with new ways of doing something is to fully test the method. For you, that may mean hours, days, weeks, or months of activity. I can't tell you how long to try something, but I can tell you if you're at a loss to connect with the activity, don't run yourself into frustration. The goal is to move forward!

A creative mindset = freedom of boundaries.

When we are in the mental flow state of playful intelligence, it's as if our creativity has a life of its own. That's when true art or creativity happens! You find the words of your story are clear and pouring from you; you're moving from one scene to another effortlessly. You find when your time is up for the day, you want to keep going. The satisfaction and sense of accomplishment is an outward glow. Playful intelligence needs some good playin' around with to become second nature, so keep those minds open and curious—especially if you write fiction novels.

Here are a few tips on how to make playful intelligence work for you:

1. **Be open to what comes next.** Don't worry about making every sentence perfect or getting every description right. As my instructor advised me, blackout your screen, or try dictation. Let the words flow and see where they take you. Try being your character, mimic them and their responses and actions.
2. **Don't be afraid to experiment.** This is your first draft, so there's no need to play it safe. Try out new things and see what works for you. No one will read this draft but you (that in and of itself should be freeing). Writing a chapter more than once is okay. Try writing a tricky scene from different points of view, or imagine alternate reactions from characters. Have someone do the opposite of what you initially thought they would in a situation and explore where that takes the story.
3. **Embrace chaos.** You can't control everything. Let the story create its own path and see where it goes. Have you ever heard someone say a character or a story had a life of its own? Embrace the option of going off script or, in our case, off the outline or plot. Let your mind wander free of your control. If this scares you, start with events from your plot and use them

as goal posts to write toward. It's your story. Don't stress yourself out. That is not the goal here.

When does the proper work begin? Because writing *is* work, right? It can't be all play—or can it?

A full novel, for example, is developed and has a plot, story structure, characters, and theme(s). So, I won't bullshit you. Writing is hard, but in the grand scheme of things, it's not neurosurgery. You can do it. You have to want to complete what you're doing, but what I find in writers, both myself, my colleagues, and clients, is everyone tries to skip a few steps to get to the execution and outcome quicker. Each writer has a timeline they work by, whether it is stated out loud or held inside. I'm not saying throw out your timeline, but instead, manage the expectations of your process accordingly. Try setting a finite timeline, as I did with my first published book. By doing that, you'll need to make sure you manage the expectations and priorities in your life, and be flexible and kind to yourself when you do need it.

Process is one of those words that was elusive to me as a new writer. How can one know what the best process is? I mean, heck, is this book going to be the one that pulls it all together for you? I hope so, but like all things, we are individuals and as such, we are complex. What works for one author doesn't necessarily work for another. The goal of this book, as stated early on, is not to be one that dictates a process, but rather one that allows you to discover a process for yourself by answering the questions posed within.

I learned that what worked for me in my first fiction book did not work for me when writing the second book. I didn't have an accountability partner or coach asking for my word count each week. My motivation waned, but I also realized that I hadn't spent enough time at the start to figure out the middle part of the story. The novelette I wrote was fast. It had existed in my head for years and I wrote it in a couple of weeks. It took until the last book in that series for me to find my writing groove and my process to become more solidified from what I learned while drafting the previous books. Learning your process is a matter of practice, and varying that practice by experimenting with new inventive methods is part of the learning. What you do for one book may be different from the process you use for another book.

The key is to keep going.

To keep playing.

Even when it feels like it's not working.

First drafts are always a mess. That's why they're called first drafts. Remember, your creative muses are waiting for you to come and play with them. So don't be afraid to get down and dirty with your first draft. The fun is in the journey and if you keep going and practice, you will make it to your destination. Trust in the process of forward momentum and your ability to get there.

You must let go of your perfectionism. Put on your playful intelligence hat and own it. Try new things and realize that each step is a step forward. Writing is not all about the word counts, it's about a completed story, memoir, or article that has a beginning, a middle, and an end.

WRITER FUEL

Some ways to increase your playful intelligence when writing include:

Writing prompts: There are many websites that offer writing prompts to get you started. Try a few to see which ones generate a spark. Check out world-building games, like *Dungeons and Dragons*[3], and use the prompt cards as story prompts.

Free writing: Pick a length of time, grab a blank page, and let your mind wander and see where it takes you. Don't worry about

making mistakes or getting stuck, just keep writing. Then after, mine the words you wrote for golden nuggets of ideas that jump out at you.

Brainstorming: Get a group of friends or fellow writers together and bounce ideas off each other. See what new and exciting ideas come out of it. Improv games are great at getting stories rolling.

Be willing to try new things and experiment with your writing. You may surprise yourself with what you're capable of. Give yourself permission to write messy and even incompletely. Now, I know when I say incomplete, a few of you are going to have heart palpitations. But listen, unless you can draft in one sitting, this is something you'll need to come to terms with. Maybe consider short or flash fiction first over a full novel. I have lots of drafts with bullet points and directions to myself to think more about a sentence or topic. Remember, give yourself permission and allow yourself to use that permission to draft messy. It's okay to delay writing scenes or parts that stump you. Forward is the direction that you want when drafting. And if you do get really stuck, try taking a break and coming back to it later with fresh eyes and a renewed mindset.

The more you play with your writing, the more creative and enjoyable it will be. So, for the sake of your writing, get out there and play!

establishing why

"Don't ask what the world needs. Ask what makes you come alive, and go do it. Because what the world needs is people who have come alive." – Howard Thurman.[1]

ONE THING that plagues many writers is what's called the **inner critic**, or what I like to call the Sassy Saboteur. It's the beast of self-doubt that says you are not good enough. It's the snarky voice in your head that says you'll never finish your book or that no one will read it anyway. It's the whiny, nasal voice that says, 'Why bother? This story has been done before and by better writers.' It's the proverbial devil-on-your-shoulder who thrives on discord and second-guessing.

You know this voice well because it's yours, as much a part of you as your nose, your ears, your little toe. I can argue against that belittling voice and show you ways I have battled and beaten my own Sassy Saboteur, but in the end, only you can silence it or even beat it.

It's so strong though, Cassie! How can I push past that Sassy Saboteur?

By tapping into that other voice that steered you to this book; the one that wants to capture and maintain the inspiration spark. The voice that says, "Yes, I am here for this! I want to write this story; it needs to be read and heard! Let's keep going!"

Discovering the Deeper Why

You can combat the Sassy Saboteur through positive self-talk and mindset activities, including our friend from the last chapter, playful intelligence. Writer communities and friends help a great deal when you're combating that negative voice in your head. Are these methods enough, though?

No. They are not enough.

Those strategies tend to be short-term solutions. They are the endorphins surging through your bloodstream after exercising. The foreplay before getting to the big event. Instead, you need an anchor, something longer lasting and stable that won't dissipate quickly. You need a reason **Why**.

My Why started as short-term because I wanted to write a story about a female teenager and her friends for my then teen daughters. I didn't want my main character to be a victim of circumstance. I wanted her to have the strength and fortitude to save herself and others without a white knight riding in on a horse to do what she was already capable of.

My rationale deepened from there because that first book was my ultimate dream, and my goal was publication. I had been taking classes and practicing with other stories. It was time for me to jump in. I had to show my family and daughters that I could, indeed, write a book while balancing it all—an active family, work, life, and writing—because when you crave something, you work for it. And the effort made me come alive.

I brought my daughters into my Why; they are a big part of my reason. However, what I was missing from this equation was *me*. I mentioned that this Why was short-term because it didn't drive me for the next book. Do you recall how I was in the pit of despair after a successful launch in 2016? I can tell you at that point, my why was all over the place. My commitment had a wandering eye for shiny new things and other stories. I was playing, but not in a direction that moved forward. I was mistaking the icing for the cake. I needed a rooted reason for why I was giving up my free time, my sleeping hours, my weekends. On a parallel route to self-discovery during this time, I discovered Simon Sinek and his book, *Start with Why*.[2]

Simon has led a movement around knowing your Why. It seems simple: you choose to write a book, you set goals, you do the work, and you finish the book, right?

Well, maybe you do. But maybe you don't, or you stumble with your next book, or your fifth, or your tenth. I stumbled. Heck, I was flat on my back.

Reading Simon's book, along with a few others, really helped me. I have a knack for pulling in other people's reasons over my own work and my own reasons. Maybe it's a parent thing, but it always takes me a while to accept what the flight attendants advise during the safety announcements—in case of an emergency or change in cabin pressure, secure your oxygen mask before helping others. Now and then, I replay Simon Sinek's TED Talk and it's like tossing gasoline on a flickering flame.

"To inspire starts with the clarity of why." – Simon Sinek[3]

It's time to discover your Why. The questions I ask below are simple and designed to help you discover your Why. Take your time on them. Revisit them and revise them. Embrace the discomfort, answer the questions, and not with what you think someone else wants you to write. Be honest; lay it all out—the good, the bad, and the ugly.

The Why Questions:

1. Why do **_you_** want to write this book?
2. What will writing this book accomplish for you?
3. What is the message or theme you are trying to tackle?
4. If you were unable to do it, or if it was taken away from you, how would you feel?

This is hard, articulating your reason for why you want to write your book. It's complicated to put into words because the part of the brain that controls emotions does not control language, so we have to work at it. When I adventured into my Why while drafting my initial book, the creative fire it produced felt good and burned hot, but proved to be a kindling flame ignited by others. It wasn't a mature campfire that could burn all night and carry me through the rest of the series, so I had to dig deeper for the fuel.

Are you still with me? Good. It may get a little uncomfortable but know that as you ask yourself these questions and really work on your responses, you will understand your Why. It's typically not something born overnight. Be patient with yourself. Kindness is not something you only give to others—give yourself some grace, too.

I grew up in a time in which women were starting to step on the glass ceiling. Not breaking it, but stepping firmly on it. My mother raised me to be independent, strong, and self-reliant. Whereas her generation was encouraged to attend college to get their M.R.S. degree (a.k.a. find a husband), my mother, the rebellious sort, elected to go to beauty school because she valued independence over the security culture of finding a man to take care of her. My mother was my early role model. She's the spirited Italian mother that raised a fiery, Irish-Italian daughter.

Why do I tell you this? Because my Why is all wrapped up in that glass ceiling and the outdated male security culture. Labels that pre-define or box you in are something I can't stand. But I am also not a fan of victimhood. You can break your own glass ceiling, that area where you feel you need a permission slip—tear it up. Women are complex and resilient and yet have been pushed down through the ages and made subservient to so many things. So, in my world influenced by my upbringing and my mother, I'm kicking and stomping that damn glass ceiling into shards. Period.

My initial Why, that spark, was to show my daughters it could be done. However, my Why and my goals are the fuel for me to keep going, to keep writing, teaching, and learning. When I poked at the questions I asked above, I realized my stories and ongoing themes follow this as well. Your Why may need to become more, so take time and really dig into these questions. Dig, dig, dig.

In my fiction writing, I twist fairy tales and fantasies. I'll always aim to create a female character who goes beyond what is expected of her whether she's the protagonist or not. I want characters who push the barriers, sometimes kicking them down. And other times, they obliterate them. Now, don't get me wrong here, I'm not a man-hater. In fact, I love my husband beyond words. He's not my savior though; he's my partner. And that's the key to my message—the Why has to come from within you to be sustaining.

When I get lost in my story and that Sassy Saboteur is telling me I'm stupid and unworthy, that I'm skirting my responsibilities to my family or friends, this broader understanding feeds my motivational fire and directs me back to the right mindset. I have my own glass ceilings to break.

To get deeper into Why, you must know the How and how it ties into your goals.

My How was completing the first book in my first series, along with it being a story of a female saving herself and others. How does the Why above add to my fire? I enjoy creating stories, developing characters, and going on an entertaining ride, as I do when I'm reading. I crave the life of an author and a writing coach. I have more stories to tell, and so much more in the publishing world that I want to experience and secretly dominate. I want to live and breathe in this industry for the second act of my life. I enjoy working with new writers by coaching and helping them find their Why and their stories. As you can see, my Why is the sum total of who I am, and my How outlines the steps of my goals. It's specific to me and is also tied to what I like to write. Your Why and How, I suspect, will be different, and they should be. They are personal and individual by nature.

"Happiness comes from what we do. Fulfillment comes from why we do it." – Simon Sinek[4]

The How Questions:

1. How will writing this story help you achieve your goals and dreams?
2. What is driving you to this story? How do you relate to it?
3. What happens if you don't write this story? Will it impact your Why or your writing goals?

Get to know yourself through the process of these questions. If you're having a difficult time, recall what you liked to do when you were a kid. Who were your mentors and why? What impressions did they make on you, positive or negative? As you reflect upon the story of your life, especially your youth, it becomes easier to pick up certain moments, patterns, or activities that hold meaning, either big or small. These may hold clues to what drives you and what you find enjoyable. Often, as adults, we think we should merely do the things that we're somehow rewarded for. It's the transactional nature of our society that often leads us to be disconnected from the things we truly love and leaves out the option of pursuit.

Think about the activities you did that made you forget the flowing of time. You probably have heard the saying, "time flies when you're having fun." Well, moments like this are what psychologists call "the flow" and what spiritualists call "connecting with the divine."

Whatever the case for you is, these activities are where your passions lie. You are fulfilling your purpose when you're doing something that energizes you, rather than something that drains your energy and leaves you feeling exhausted.

So, Cassie, how does this help with my Sassy Saboteur?

Say you're having a bad day. Things aren't going well. Everything you're doing is crap. How does your Why bring you back around?

Well, it's not something you just pick out of the air, throw into your subconscious, and suddenly everything is flowing.

Let's be realistic about how things work. I recommend doing what I referred to earlier in the book.

Step away

Breathe

Try something else

My Why is important enough that I'm not just going to drop the pen, shut down my computer, walk away, and never return. Although, it happens, people do walk away never to return. They start off with the best of intentions, and maybe one day they'll resurface to complete them. And it's not to say their Why is any less than yours, but it's not motivating them, and it's not their current priority. If you are motivated to finish your book, if this is your priority, you will come back because your Why is deep, profound, and it centers you. Essentially, it's your mission statement, a mantra for the work you are doing.

What you shouldn't do is allow the Why discovery to slow down the start of your writing. Keep developing your Why as you go, because your Why will evolve. Forward momentum is the goal. Keep going. Your fire is lit, you now know your Why and your How. These components are what fuels your motivational and inspirational fire.

disconnection and creativity

THERE ARE many theories about where creativity comes from and what it actually is. Some people believe that creativity is a divine gift, while others think it is something that can be learned and cultivated. Personally, I believe it's a bit of both. In my experience, writing is something I've learned through reading, courses, and craft books. However, that said, how I put it all to use is something I have been cultivating for more than a decade.

Here's the deal, regardless of creativity being thought of as a gift or a learned activity, you have to apply it to your goal, otherwise, what's the benefit? Once you identify that creative state within you, harness it and practice. Learn more—do more.

I don't have the best gift for literary storytelling, but I enjoy fast-moving stories and solid character growth. I practice by writing dialogue and fast story plots that hook readers and keep them turning the page. These are the natural components of storytelling for me to focus on because it's what I enjoy reading and emulating. Writing what you like and enjoy reading is a great first step. But it's just that, one small step—we want to leap! Use your favorite authors and stories for your muses, use them as fuel. If you don't have a favorite author or story, no worries, figure out what is driving you, as mentioned earlier in this book, name it and use it, build upon it. Don't let the Sassy Saboteur in; there's no room for judgment.

One of the most popular theories about creativity is the idea of **incubation**. This theory suggests that creativity comes from a process of subconscious thought. During incubation, you allow your mind to wander away, and you don't focus on trying, or solving the problem at hand.

Incubation involves taking a break from your work, or by stepping away from it completely. For me, this is taking a proper break from a story and working on something else before coming back to the original story. Time away from anything produces a result. This change of scenery or focus can help to reset your mind and give you a new perspective on how to approach a creative task or potential issue. After being away for a bit, you may find that the answer you were searching for was staring you in the face all along!

WRITER FUEL

"Others have seen what is and asked why. I have seen what could be and asked why not." – Pablo Picasso[1]

The most important thing to remember with creativity is that it requires a certain mindset to take root and grow.

Utilize disconnection to be creative

Creativity is all about seeing the world in a new way, and that is hard to do when your head is full of distractions. When you're constantly bombarded with emails, texts, and phone calls, it's tough to focus on anything else. That's why it's important to take a break from technology and other social pulls—to give your brain a chance to rejuvenate. Disconnecting can help you come up with new ideas and better solutions to plot problems or character issues, and fosters a clarity of thought.

Plus, stepping away can make you more productive when you finally sit back down at your desk. You'll clearly see what needs to be done, and you'll be less likely to get sidetracked by trivial tasks. Disconnect from writing now and then, and see what new ideas and solutions you come up with!

If this is your first time trying this technique, start by disconnecting for thirty minutes to an hour. See how you feel afterward—do you have a new perspective on the problem? Are you any closer to a solution? If not, try disconnecting for a full day or even longer.

The important thing is to be flexible and find what length of time or alternate activity works best for you. Think about what grounds you when you feel anxious or need comfort. For some it could be going outdoors, exercise, or meditation—possibly all three even. For me, having thirty minutes away can be enough time to reset.

I can do a chore around my house or watch a favorite television show during that time, and it helps me rebalance. The point of disconnection is to return and see what's in front of you in a new way, with a clear mind after some time away from your task at hand.

Creativity takes practice.

Let me say that again, creativity takes practice.

When I coach a new writer who is struggling, or the scene I'm writing isn't quite right, frustration and anxiety often loom overhead like dark shadows. The technique I recommend to sweep away the shadows is to rewrite the scene.

Practice for me meant I rewrote many chapters and scenes in *Reign*, my second fiction novel. I had action scenes that didn't always flow well. I had perspectives and knowledge I needed to impart for proper transitional sequences that didn't always connect. The process of rewriting allowed me to try different things, explore new angles, and use alternate character reactions. And, yes, some brilliant a-ha moments resulted, including a surprise character death and rebirth that I hadn't planned on. We are talking about big, plot changing events here! There were several of those moments when I allowed myself to rewrite and let the pen and paper takeover (i.e., creative transference—I'll talk more on what that is below). Following the completion of the series, *Reign* remains my favorite book not only for the story, but the struggle and the improvement the creative practice gave me. These are the things our readers may never know about us

—the practice and the struggle—but they help us grow in our writing.

Overcoming creative blocks

There is an idea that you must mold and shape the first words you write into perfection as soon as they hit the paper. This is often unrealistic. Drafting your initial idea is a framework, it's like clay, and it's moldable. You may have a specific process, but if you're stuck, try this for me —pause that process.

This approach of pausing involves taking a step back from your work to get a fresh perspective on it. You may struggle with plot holes and other creative blocks, but you don't want to get to the point where you give up. This is where a mindset-rebooting technique can come in handy. Taking a break from the task at hand, or stepping away from it entirely, truly helps. I love having a good nap to clear the cobwebs and fill in the ruts I'm stuck in.

Okay, Cassie, I took the break. But now what?

Time to be repetitive. This is an exercise to expand the creative outlet of the problem at hand. Begin by asking yourself prompting questions such as 'What if?' or 'and then...' and begin to free write (sans judgment) those answers. Recognize frustration as an indicator of the need to reboot and refresh your mindset. It's the prime time to reconnect with the fuel of your fire for writing this story in the first place.

Don't start over and rewrite everything, though. Be strategic here and find the pain points. Be objective. Is it one scene or a specific chapter that pulls the others out of whack? Then let's *practice* to solve the issue.

What? Practice?

Yes, rewriting is practice. Editing is practice. It's super rare for writers to draft, then do one round of edits and hit publish. If that effortless scenario is in your head— throw it out and get rid of it. You, my friend, are not the rare diamond, and neither am I; well, at least not in that scenario.

"You can never solve a problem on the level on which it was created." – Albert Einstein[2]

Once you have these troublesome pain points, let's say, scenes identified, rewrite them a minimum of three times and no more than five times, with a fifteen-to-twenty-minute break in between. Each iteration must be on a separate blank page or if you're dictating, open a new recording and new transcription. Each session should be clear of the last, which is why having a new paper or document is important. Have the idea of what needs to occur in your scene in your mind, however, keep it loose. It's a framework—remember the moldable clay.

Give yourself a reasonable time limit to rewrite each of these three scenes with the break noted above between each. If it needs to carry over into days instead of hours, plan so it can be consecutive days (the why of which I'll explain shortly).

Creative blocks can be frustrating and debilitating, but with the right mindset techniques, you can overcome them and get back to finishing your draft!

Begin by relaxing your shoulders and unclenching your jaw. Now, for the rewrites with twists and new options; the goal is not to mirror the old scene. You want these versions to be new and fresh. Remember earlier when I mentioned we would work with scene rewrites later? Here is that chance.

Carry out each point below for your chosen story component (scene, chapter, conversation, etc.) with abandon and the full interaction of your cast of characters:

- Write from a new point of view—instead of first person, write from third person.
- Write from a different character's point of view and in their unique voice.
- Move the setting to a new place or change the location completely.
- Add in an event that wasn't there before or remove an event.
- Have a character respond opposite to what is expected.

What does this do? It helps to get you out of your block, and nine times out of ten, writers are happier with their most recent exercise. The reason for this is what I call **creative transference**. Creative transference is a redirection of what your mind is subconsciously molding into the next scene and the one after that. You're building up a mechanism of practice with your scene in the first round; by the second rewrite, you're getting the hang of it, and bits from each attempt are weaving into your brain subconsciously (the transference part). By the third or the last round, you've latched onto the creative flow and it's the authentic story thread that lands on the page.

The beauty of this exercise is that you are doing three important things:

1. You are facing the issue without judgment head-on.
2. You are practicing the scene and story by testing with no commitment.
3. You are allowing your creative brain the space to process and solve the issue at hand.

You have disconnected!

Creativity is practice. The more you write, the more you practice, the more attaining your creative flow state becomes second nature. Does practice make perfect? No. Practice in this case makes improvement.

The best way to solve a problem is to work at it. Does it suck sometimes to rewrite something five times? Yep, sure does, but it beats staring at an issue in your story for several months with no forward progress. Being stuck only defeats you, and you can stagnate for days that become weeks, which can become months or even years. Practice and rewriting generate and maintain forward momentum.

The secret to keeping motivation high is to work on the thing that will get you to your goals. If you stop without recourse to return, your motivation will wane. Have you ever heard it takes twenty-one days to form a habit? I believe there is some merit to this principle, but what is more lucrative is a plan. If you need to walk away—walk away but have a plan to return. If it's a one-week, non-writing sabbatical you decide on, then on day eight, come back and start to work, ahem, I mean play; play is work, remember? No one loves coming back to work from vacation, so flip that mindset.

All progress is forward momentum, and that includes disconnection. It's not a bad thing to disconnect occasionally, in fact, it can be a reward unto itself. The advice within the writing world that you must write daily works for some, but in my experience, it hinders me more than it helps. If you've been writing daily and you love it, keep doing it.

For those that struggle with a blinking cursor and tears that include a demotivation cloud hanging over your head, take the sabbatical, and try attaining mindset in which disconnection equals creativity.

quitting vs. a sticking tactic vs. a strategy

YOU MAY NOT BE ready to hear this, but it's time to talk about quitting.

What? Why?

Isn't this book about holding a motivational spark from the beginning to the end and completing a first draft?

Yes, it is. But it's also a kick in the ass to determine when you need to quit, pivot, or plow through. I'm not going to sugarcoat it for you because you need to be able to recognize what's going on with your motivation as you go through your writing process.

What I find is, if you know all the options and can get a feel for the journey from this book, you are better armed to make the decision about which path to take, especially when to push through and, if needed, when to pivot. This chapter aims to illuminate and define these pathways.

Quitting can be the best thing you do for yourself. It allows you to move on and accept what you don't want in order to pursue what you do. For example, you could start on the wrong story idea, or, as you begin to refine your process, you learn that you need more research or plotting. This type of quit is called a **pivot**. It's trading one thing for another. If you ask any writer, there are stories and full novels sitting in drawers and on computer drives that will never see the light of day. Part of the reason for this is an exercise in pivoting.

The Pivot Approach

I have a 90k word fantasy novel on my computer drive that I recently revisited. At the beginning of drafting this story, my intended goal was to finish it. I even took a class to help me plan and push through

obstacles on the way to writing 'The End.' It's not the most horrible piece of writing imaginable, parts of it have some merit. The most valuable aspect of this manuscript, however, is what I learned from that writing experience. That draft taught me that—say it with me—**practice doesn't make perfection, it makes improvement.**

Once I finished, I realized I didn't want to revise and edit that manuscript. I had no desire to go back over those 90k words again, never mind multiple times. I recognized that was my moment to pivot because I knew my goal wasn't to publish that story, it was only to complete the first draft. I continued my writing education and practice by composing short stories and poems, and I took a class on writing screenplays. Essentially, the new goal I pivoted to was to find my fit (on type of story and genre) and to discover the next story worthy of writing and publishing. When that story spark ignited in my mind, I was prepared to write it and publish it then. I was all in, and that was how *Magick*, my debut novel, was born.

Magick's origin is an example of how quitting on my very first story not only became a pivot for me, but also a strategy. Quitting can be liberating because it brings you closer to accepting what you don't want. And sometimes you don't know what you want until you try. At some point, that naysaying devil, the Sassy Saboteur (if you have one), will also raise its voice and question your drive, confidence, knowledge, and maybe even your dedication. *You can't do this. It's too tough—you should just quit.* But there is a difference between a full-on quit and acknowledging that maybe you just need to pivot.

There is no shame in quitting outright or pivoting.

Quitting is when you give up on something completely, while pivoting is when you change your approach by trading one focus for another. If you're feeling stuck in your project, you may want to consider pivoting before abandoning the work you've done.

Here are some tips for pivoting:

- Identify the problem and categorize it.
- Come up with a fresh approach to solving the problem.
- Act on the new approach.
- Evaluate the results.

If you find that your new approach isn't working, it's okay to quit. There is no shame. You are allowed to change your mind. The goal is to know when it's a phase to push through, when to pay attention in order to decide on the next steps, or if it's a full stop.

WRITER FUEL

The Quit Approach

Cassie, how do I know if it's a full stop—a complete quit moment?

This is a tough question to answer and is individual to you. I recommend phrasing your goal in terms of what you want to achieve short-term versus long-term. Refrain from comparing your past with your present. Forward-looking only, please!

I say this because the past can drown you in unnecessary noise. I had a relative tell me I let my girls quit too many activities when they were young. Once they completed their term of gymnastics, soccer, volleyball, ballet, violin, and even martial arts, I didn't push for them to keep going if they didn't want to. To me, it's discovery, not quitting, and if you base your decision on having quit things in the past, then you're stuck in the past and not moving forward. Don't stick it out because you fear someone will call you a quitter. No schoolyard games here. This is your life. Own it. Today and tomorrow, you have a clean slate for this decision. Mustering your purposeful intent is now. Practice is now. Don't allow the past to take up residence in a room you didn't invite it into. Take your time in thinking through what you genuinely want.

Here are a few different things you can do to help you decide on whether to quit:

- Ask yourself if it's a phase or something *you* really don't want.
- Weigh the pros and cons of quitting against your 'why.'
- Talk to someone about your decision—they may give you some helpful advice.

The Pause Approach

Sometimes, quitting is the best decision, and other times it is not. Quitting is something you should think through thoroughly, especially if you dreamed of holding your stories as published books in your hands. But if all your options to pivot and momentum-regaining methods have been exhausted, then maybe this is a way forward for you. Quitting doesn't always have to mean giving up on something forever; sometimes it means taking a solid break from whatever project or task has become overwhelming to get back into gear later with renewed energy, creativity, and a plan.

Quitting can also simply be a way of saying "no" to something that isn't serving you to make space for something that will. Trust your gut and listen to what it is telling you. If you feel like quitting, there is probably a good reason. Quitting is not always easy, but it can be worth it in the long run if it's what you truly want.

Don't make quitting easy, make it a hard decision.

Quitting is not failure, it's a responsibility to yourself and your life goals.

Your decision to quit is not a slogan or a tagline for others to mock.

As with anything in your life, it's your decision and you shouldn't be fearful of judgment. I'm here to tell you if you need or want to quit writing your story—it's okay. You are not harming yourself; you are supporting yourself and your desires at this point in time. I support you because that's what people should do over passing judgment. Take comfort in this book. The motivational side of your decision is the courage to quit something you've been struggling with and pushing against when you know you're done with it.

If you are just starting, knowing that you have options such as pivoting, pausing, and quitting is beneficial. These are tactics you can employ; it's not failure, it's a strategy. You make the choice of whether quitting is permanent or temporary.

Now that you're more motivated than ever by the permission to change your mind and goals, let's get to the next chapter on how to support the trials of writing the first draft of your novel.

zigging and zagging

IT'S normal to get off the path of writing a book, especially if it's not something you've ever done before. We're only human, after all, and the path of least resistance will always be the most attractive route. This type of behavior is what I call **zigging and zagging**. It happens all the time with writers. Zigging is getting off track, whereas zagging is getting back on it. Some might call it to-and-fro. You get the idea.

It's easy to get off course when you're drafting your story. Sometimes you might find yourself stuck, unsure of where to go next. Other times, you may make a mistake and want to start over. The takeaway here is that you ultimately get back into your story in whatever form that takes to maintain forward progress.

It's worthwhile to take a moment and figure out what led you astray in the first place. Identifying the new draw can be difficult to do, but it's crucial if you are struggling to get back on the momentum train, and more importantly, to recognize the signs of stumbling to avoid derailing in the future. Once you have identified the root cause of why you fell off course, you can then take steps to correct or prevent it next time. In some cases, this may mean changing your entire approach.

Here are a few techniques to help you get back on track and moving forward on your story and toward your goals:

Make a plan. This can include outlining your story before you start writing, or coming up with a list of scenes, actions, chapters, etc., that you aim to write for the day. Having a plan in place will help you stay on track and avoid getting stuck.

My plan begins with the end. I always know how I want the book to end, so I start there. I begin by writing the first chapter and last chapters before anything else. These two pieces act as the goal posts of my plan, and in the case of the last chapter, a destination to work toward. Next, I lay down beats (short descriptive paragraphs) to figure out my story skeleton in between the goal posts.

With this plan in place, I can begin drafting. I write the draft in a multifaceted writing program called Scrivener; [1] its structure allows me to move entire scenes, chapters, and large blocks of text around easily.

Do the first and last chapters change? Most definitely, especially during the editing process. I've been known to scrap a first chapter completely, but not until I've finished my initial, full story draft. Remember the key is forward momentum.

What I mean by that is that I plow through

my draft until all the skeleton beats are now scenes and full chapters. I call this planning process **skinny drafting** because it produces a draft that is skinny word-wise compared to what it will be, but the relevant structure is there. The idea behind skinny drafting is to start with the basic components of a scene (beats) and build from there, adding descriptions and layers, weaving in details, and constructing settings until eventually, it becomes the first draft. For me, this keeps the story interesting. Skinny drafting allows me time to think over subsequent scenes within a framework that is clear and easy to amend.

As additional motivation, I put a timeline to this process. I allow myself three rounds to draft, and then I move on to edits and revisions. This way I'm not stuck in a loop of perpetual drafting.

Take breaks. If you find yourself stuck, it can help to take a break and come back to your story later. This can help refresh your mind and give you a new perspective on your work. I realize almost every chapter says take a break, but it is essential to renewing your perspective and rallying your thoughts.

I look at breaks as an option to either quiet my mind or over-fuel my mind. It's one of two streets for me. Quieting my mind may look like taking a nap, meditation, relaxing in the bath, or even that greatest of mindless activities, cleaning. Over-fueling is when I purposefully jam to music, dance it out, or watch a favorite movie loud to drown out the mind noise.

Yup, that's right, I dance it out with complete abandon, think a mix between a concert goer and pretending I'm on JLo's dance crew... and it's amazing for clearing away the mire. That simple, fun bout of exercise frees my brain by focusing on the music and gets my body moving (for the *Grey's Anatomy*[1] fans, you know what I mean!). Try it!

Dancing isn't the only way to engage in over-fueling, any other type of vigorous exercise you enjoy can work just as well. Make it an active break and you will return to your story with a clearer mind.

Prioritize your time. Make writing a priority in your life, and schedule time for it accordingly. This can help you stay on track and make progress with your work. Setting a

deadline for finishing your draft can also help motivate you to keep writing and avoid getting sidetracked.

I use an electronic planner on my iPad through a notebook application called GoodNotes.[2] I love it. I keep only my writing goals and deadlines in it, along with various inspirations. I list my different writing projects and their individual tasks with check boxes that I love ticking off as I complete them. That small action in itself is energizing and keeps me moving on to the next item. The list directs my forward progress.

Do I miss tasks? You bet I do, but I love the electronic planner because I can cut and paste and move things around as I need to (flexibility is the key for me).

I plan by year, quarter, month, and I plot my week. I take time each Sunday to reflect on where I am for the week ahead and adjust my tasks as necessary, with moving forward as the goal. It's my quiet time, and it motivates me. I think about what went well and what cool things happened over the week. When I'm particularly down, I review further into the past and I'm always amazed at what I have accomplished.

Join a writing group. Being part of a group or community provides accountability and support as you work on drafting your story. Asking for feedback from fellow writers or a critique partner can help you when you're off track. Not all writing groups are equal, but I've been fortunate to meet some wonderful people along the way in a couple of different groups. The support and confidence you receive from such communities are beyond words invaluable.

Finding a group to join can seem daunting, however, there are usually writers' groups based in your local area. Try doing a Google search with a set radius and checking out your local library for contacts as well. These days you can often join groups in other states, countries, even time zones because of the growth of electronic meeting platforms and social media. The world is now much more accessible and interacting with like-minded people is a valuable tool for any writer.

"Everyone falls down. Getting back up is how you learn how to walk." – Walt Disney[3]

Free Writing. Another option, when you are stagnant and noticing frustration building, is to try **free writing**. Free writing is a nonsensical approach to writing without purpose and allows your subconscience to take over. I have a friend who does free writing for ten minutes prior to ever touching her story. Sometimes there are story bits unearthed, and other times it's just stuff she's getting out of her head to free up creative space.

I do this same exercise when dictating (my favorite way to start my second-round drafts). I have to mentally gear up for this draft because it's a little awkward to talk non-stop to yourself. I get comfortable by 'free talking' about anything for ten minutes prior to opening the manuscript. Something magical happens in these free writing sessions. Your inhibitions loosen up and the floodgates open. Words flow easily and you can transfer that momentum to your story composition. If you feel stuck, give free writing or dictation a try.

Getting back on track is tough but so are you

In my experience as a writing coach and an author, I've seen many writers (both published and unpublished) go through different struggles with their manuscripts.

Many of these struggles come from a lack of self-confidence or certainty in their work. As a result, these writers often doubt their writing ability and give up on their project prematurely. Try to commit to your work and trust in the process that you are doing what you are supposed to be doing to finish your book in whatever time frame you've established.

When you think about all the commitments you have in your life, shouldn't *you* be one of them? Shouldn't your story and writing be a commitment?

Then make sure you are setting yourself up for success.

When you decide to start working out, you put on your running shoes, your workout clothes, and grab a water bottle. You're not ready to run a marathon, but you are ready to start day one, then progress to the next day as you build up your muscles and cardiovascular health. Before too long, you're ready to go for that first big challenge: the 3k, 5k, etc. I feel that the same is true for writing.

If you find yourself getting off track, don't fret and fall down a self-deprecating pit of despair. You're not unique in this; a lot of writers zig and zag. The important action is zagging and getting back on track.

There is a rare beauty in getting off track. I discovered it when writing my second book. If you recall from earlier, I had a two-year break between my first and second novels. I tried a couple of different starts on book two even before the shiny new story came in, and that alone deterred me. However, I managed to get back on track by making the decision first, and then putting together my plan, I began to play, and I found the right start for that story. In hindsight, I wouldn't change a thing, but at the time, I was spinning in a circle. I obviously needed the break.

"...if you want the rainbow, you gotta put up with the rain!"
— Dolly Parton[4]

Writing is hard; it's not for the uncommitted. Be committed to yourself and this goal of finishing your draft. And keep these techniques in mind the next time you are trying to zag your way back on track.

The number one way to hold yourself accountable is to find someone with whom to share your progress or lack thereof. Reporting to a real, living person who can offer feedback helps most people stay motivated because they don't want their peers or loved ones to know that they're not meeting their goals.

When you feel like giving up, try calling up your writing partner or writing group members and telling them about your struggles. Fellow writers are the best support agents because they've most likely been there and can talk you through some solutions or offer a friendly ear. If you don't have a community, look into working with a book or writing coach who holds accountability sessions. You may find that having someone to be accountable to and who will hold you to a schedule is just the push you need to break through the block.

If the above sounds awful to you, you could be more internally motivated. It may be a plan with a to-do list that propels you, where you can check off your completion of the set day's, week's, or month's activities. The internal motivation to get back on track is a personal one that only you can design.

I do recommend that you are kind and graceful to yourself, though. Too many times, we come back from a break or struggle and expect that getting back to where we were months ago should look and feel the same as when we started. This is a mistake because you're no longer ready for the marathon; your muscles are not primed for that. You've got to train for it again—maybe not from a day-one-starting condition, but don't discount the possibility.

Remember that drafting is not editing. Drafting is all about you telling yourself the story, from beginning to end. You and your editor can and will add, subtract, and fine-tune your story during the editing process. But once you have completed all the scenes and chapters in your first draft and put them into an order that makes sense—guess what?

You have finished your draft, my friend!

You have done the hardest work and written your story!

the beauty of finished

YOU HAVE TYPED 'THE END'—AND it is an unwritten writer's rule that you must physically put the words at the end of your story. Why? Because it's a huge accomplishment and nothing says that better than 'The End.' The goal of your story has been achieved. It is no longer a brief idea or a want; it's an accomplishment, a reality.

Your draft is finished!

You started before you were ready. You did the work and played along the way. You named the spark, defined the Why, and identified the How. You picked up some tools for managing the expectations and setbacks you had along the way. You were able to zig and zag all the way to a completed story draft!

Celebrate the moment you complete your draft. Don't wait until you publish or finish your edits. Celebrate this major milestone. Be proud of yourself each step of the way to reaching the ultimate goal. Each little celebration gives a sense of accomplishment and motivates you to keep going. You crossed the finish line, whether it be your first or your tenth. Without celebrations during the journey, it would be easy to lose sight of our goals and give up on our dreams.

In fact, write down how you will celebrate; make the commitment. Don't make this a last-minute joyous thing, make a deal with yourself for what you will do. My celebrations are anywhere from a nice dinner at a restaurant to a pedicure and manicure, a spa day, or a full-on vacation out of town.

This girl knows how to reward herself. Don't be shy here. Make your reward count as something you want and will relish in receiving. Make it part of the finishing motivation. Part of the fuel for your writing fire.

There is beauty in completion, the raising of a glass in toast to your own hard work. It is a thing of wonder, this journey we take from blank page to full story. It's something you made and crafted all from your mind and creativity. It's uniquely yours and your voice. This particular practice round is over. Can you believe it?

"Knowledge is a treasure but practice is the key to it." – *Lao Tzu*[1]

Every finished story is a practice round for the next (especially if more than one story is your long-term goal). There is no perfection in story writing. When you finish your first draft, you should feel proud of yourself because it means you've done the hardest part: you've laid down the bones of the story. Now it's time to revise, edit, and polish it until it shines.

The best way to stay motivated and inspired during the revision and editing process is to remember why you wrote the story in the first place. Revisit the Why section when you need to and remember, revise the reason Why to go deeper when you need it to evolve with your purpose of writing in general or for the book directly. It's your internal writer flame that drives you, not only to draft but to finish your edits; that burning desire to hold that physical book in your hands.

Cassie Newell

"To write is human, to edit is divine." – Stephen King[2]

The revision and editing stage generates polarized opinions among writers. Some love it and others can't be done with it fast enough.

The key to staying motivated is to set realistic goals for yourself during this stage. Don't revise the entire story in a single sitting; break it down into smaller tasks that you can complete. Editing may feel daunting, but it's important to remember that every writer feels this way at some point. Just take it one step at a time and be patient with yourself.

Begin with small steps in the revision process by doing the following:

- Start with global, big-picture revisions, such as plot, character, or pacing.
- Then move on to examine and polish details, like word choice, language, and sentence structure.
- Finally, inspect spelling and grammar before proofreading the final product and sending to an editor.

I have a three-editing-pass rule for myself per the above points. And the reason is that I might stay in a self-editing loop without ever seeing a novel finished. I found myself in this situation while writing *Magick*, and my writing coach at the time asked me whether I wanted to be perfect or did I want to be published? The purpose of asking me that question was to point out that no book, in the millions of books out there, is perfect. So, I needed to develop a revision process that allows me to disengage and accept that at a certain point; the story is where it needs to be for the next practice round to proceed.

I finished my first novel for publication in 2016, and when I saw negative reviews, I kicked myself with the self-talk of the *could have-should have* debate. Meaning, I wanted to go back and revise my first book immediately! I wanted to address those reviews. I had to ask myself why, because, after all, I had won an award for *Magick*, so therefore someone thought it was great, right? Isn't it funny how we gravitate toward the negative over the positive 100 times over?

Later, when I was ready to tackle the rest of the series, I held the fact that I finished my first book, and the knowledge that I could repeat the achievement, in my back pocket.

There is a sense of achievement when you know you've done something before. Yes, each book is its own brand of special, but knowing you've worn the shoes and traveled the path before is comforting, regardless of if it is a hit with readers, ranking charts, or award-winning or not. This is my practice, not my perfection.

Then I poured my energy into my second, third, and fourth books. In each book, I learned more and more about my process. Because here is the deal: you don't know your process until you practice and write more and more and more. What is natural, what works, and what doesn't work is different for each writer.

Try to be flexible when you're stuck in your own process as well. The reason I say this is that your process will evolve from book to book, with little tweaks here and there. How I draft has changed for me over time. I learned that for me, collaboration and discussion are important for my process. I also learned I love that part of being a writing coach.

With practice comes familiarity

There is a security blanket aspect to finishing your first book, because with the second one, you know you can do it because you have done it before.

You will continue to develop your craft and keep going because it's only upward from here. It's not the end because there is no perfection in story writing. There is only the next story and the one after that. Each one is a practice round for the next book. So, keep writing, keep learning, and most importantly, keep celebrating your finished stories—because you made it!

You are now an author.

a sassy mindset

"The most common way people give up their power is by thinking they don't have any." – Alice Walker[1]

MAINTAINING a creative mindset can be difficult, but it's worth the effort. By taking the time to learn about and practice different creative techniques for building and fueling your motivational fire to finish your story, you increase your chances of success. This book was designed not only to help you through the draft of the first story, but to help you for your next, if that is your goal—which it should be! Writing stories contributes to culture through providing entertainment, lessons in humanity, and the expansion of empathy in our world. And stories are just damn fun!

So many people talk about writing a story. The fact is, talk is fleeting because not everyone truly intends to write a story. You, however, by buying this book and actively working through the questions asked, are burning to make that happen!

Enlisting a great support system at home that values your goals and dreams is crucial to your success. Sometimes there will be naysayers because, well, there always are; not everyone is going to be supportive. If you're one of the lucky ones that bathes in support all around you, that is wonderful. Use it and be grateful for it. Not all are so lucky.

What do you do if you don't have enthusiastic external support? You become your own support system. This is the Sassy Mindset. Be hardheaded in your pursuit of what you want.

There are a couple of ways to become your own support:

1. Pure will-power and wrapping yourself in your Why.
2. Allowing the story to drive you beyond your fear of not finishing it.
3. Persisting because you have no plan B; this is it or you'll be miserable otherwise.
4. To show the naysayers you can. Because screw them.

Are the above ways the only way? Um, hells no. But this is what I have experience in.

When I was younger (middle school), I struggled to make good grades. I had a teacher who took me aside and asked me a couple of questions. She asked if the material was hard. I said no. She asked me why I wasn't committed to learning, to which I shrugged. I must have made a face of irritation because she asked if I liked her as a teacher. I was shocked, to be honest, because no, I did not, and I answered so as politely as I could. She called my parents. I was in trouble, and all my free time was taken away. My life was miserable because, at twelve, the sky is falling when you're in trouble with no freedoms.

Although I don't remember that teacher's name, I remember her smiling and saying, if I wanted to get back at her—really stick it to her—I could work hard enough to force her to do the most uncomfortable thing: to give me a passing, or even an excellent grade. Failing me was no skin off her back because that would make her right about me. But if I did what I was supposed to and earned a higher grade, I'd have proven her wrong. My sassy young ass took this as the ultimate rebellion against this teacher. Besides, I had no free time and rebelling by pouting would not serve this dish of making her grade me as excellent. I would not let her put me in a box because I didn't hand in my homework or pass a couple of tests. She didn't know me.

Needless to say, I made her give me that excellent grade. Little did I understand at the time, but she was guiding me to reprogram my mindset so I would achieve a better outcome. She reframed my rebellion into productivity.

The purpose of this story is to demonstrate that you can be hard-wired one way for a particular outcome, either positive or negative, and in which case, you will always have that outcome. When people talk about mindset, I watch them fall into one of two categories, doubt or fear, especially if they are new to the concept of doubt and fear, i.e., the Sassy Saboteur.

Doubt will always be there, from the little nagging stabs to the big gun anxiety of failure. We all have it in some form or another.

Fear is challenging but also healthy because it drives you to put your best foot forward. But it can cripple you if you don't deal with it or recognize when it's taking over. Fear is something you either run or rise from. In the writing world, it usually involves self-talk comparing yourself to other authors. Remember you're playing for **yourself**, not Stephen King or some other author you admire. Please stop comparing your very first timeline and story to someone who has years of experience. I'm not saying get rid of your fear, but I am saying stop comparing, stop the what if's, their fire is different from yours. Tend to *your* writer fire instead.

Focus on your next goals, both short-term and long-term. It may be a better character arc, writing in a new genre, or ranking in a book category for sales. Or if you're like me, my long-terms goals are to be featured in a book subscription box and to receive the best seller ranking one day. Are these things going to hold me back if I don't achieve them? No. Because I'm practicing and so are you. Each step is another achievement toward my long-term goals, which like life, are ever-evolving.

"Motivation will almost always beat mere talent." – Norman Ralph Augustine[2]

It's a process to get into a mindset that maintains that writer fire. I designed each chapter of this book in a way to get these mindset concepts and tools into your arsenal to call upon as you need them. Motivation and inspiration are tricky because building and maintaining them are individual processes. It's not a one-size-fits-all concept.

This is just the beginning for you, dear writer, I feel it! Keep practicing and practicing. It's all within your power to reach your goals with your completed story, whether that be publication to the masses, as a gift to a loved one, or to live in your desk drawer to prove you could finish it. Be your own best advocate for what motivates you. Fan the flames that you are building and let that fire burn everlasting!

mindset review

AS A BONUS, below is a quick summary of the different mindset techniques I spoke about throughout this book:

Label it: Actions cause reactions. Light that fire with the spark of your idea for the story. Make it tangible.

Start and make your goal: Begin. Whatever the 'start' is for you—get to it. Make it simple. (Remember, you don't have to know everything before you begin.)

Drafting is playing: Adopt playful intelligence to enjoy what you are drafting. Writing is messy, and that is okay, accept it!

Know your Why: Secure your goals with your personal, deep-rooted reason for writing this story. Revisit and pressure test your reason by knowing how to accomplish your Why.

Protect your creativity: Creativity takes practice. Try new things if you are stuck either internally or externally. Have patience with yourself.

You can change your mind: Quitting is not failure, it's all in your hands and is your choice. Take the opportunity to rest or step away when you need to and reset toward your goal when you come back.

Prioritize you: Protect your time to write and make plans. Find your writing community and tribe. Writing doesn't have to be a solo activity.

Finish it: Practice does not mean perfect. Practice makes improvements. Keep practicing!

author's note

Dear Reader,

Thank you for taking the time to read *Writer Fuel*. My hope is that you've learned something and it helps you in your writing journey.

Your extra goodies, make sure to download:

- Free Writer Fuel Companion Workbook
- Free Develop Your Idea To A Story Premise

   www.sassywritingcoach.com/extrafuel

A final note, if you've enjoyed this book, please consider leaving a review at your retailer. Reviews are the lifeblood of independent authors, and I can't thank you

Author's Note

enough for showing other readers what you thought of the book. Even a quick star rating can go a loooong way.

Until next time.

Be well & stay sassy,

Cassie

Did this book have an impact?

Tell me your story!

bibliography

1989. *Advanced Dungeons & Dragons: Player's Handbook.* Vol. 2nd Edition. Random House.
Anthony T. DeBenedet, M.D. 2018. *Playful Intelligence: The Power of Living Lightly in a Serious World.* Santa Monica Press, LLC.
Augustine, Norman R. 1986. *Augustine's Laws.* American Institute of Aeronautics and Astronautics Inc., Viking.
2005. *Grey's Anatomy.* Directed by Adam Davidson. Performed by Sandra Oh, Ellen Pompeo.
Gaspirtz, Oliver. 2016. *German Wisdom: Funny, inspirational, and thought-provoking quotes by famous Germans.* Westhoff Publishing.
Godin, Seth. 2004. *How to Make a Purple Cow.* Penguin.
2022. "GoodNotes." GoodNotes Limited.
Gretzky, Wayne, interview by Bob McKenzie. 1983. *The Hockey News*
King, Stephen. 2002. *On Writing: A Memoir of the Craft.* Pocket Books.
Laozi Wu Jingxiong, Ching TAo Teh. 1990. *Lao Tzu Quotes.* Shambhala.
Martin, William P. 2004. *The Best Liberal Quotes Ever: Why the Left is Right.* Sourcebooks.
Nuance. 2022. "Dragon Anywhere." Nuance Communications, Inc.
2022. "Otter.ai." Otter.ai, Inc.
Parton, Dolly. 2013. *Twitter.* April 4. Accessed May 2022. https://twitter.com/dollyparton/status/319869370727796736
Picasso, Pablo. n.d. *Pablopicasso.org/quotes.* Accessed August 13, 2022. https://www.pablopicasso.org/quotes.jsp.
2022. "Scrivener." Literature & Latte Ltd.
Sinek, Simon. 2017. *Find Your Why: A Practical Guide For Discovering Purpose For You and Your Team.* Penguin.
—. 2009. *Start With Why: How Great Leaders Inspire Everyone To Take Action.* Penguin.
Sreechinth, C. 2016. *The Vault of Walt Disney Quotes: Best Walt Disney Quotes.* UB Tech.

Bibliography

Thurman, Howard. 1980. "The Sound of the Genuine." Spelman College Commencement Address.

Waldschmidt, Daniel E. 2014. *Edgy Conversations: How Ordinary People Achieve Outrageous Success.* Made For Success, Inc.

Wetzel, Stephanie and Charlie. 2020. *The Spanx Story. Sara Blakely.* HarperCollins Leadership.

2002. *Sweet Home Alabama.* Directed by Andy Tennant. Performed by Reese Witherspoon.

endnotes

2. Name It before You Start It

1. (Godin 2004)

3. Start before You Are Ready

1. (Gretzky 1983)
2. (Wetzel 2020)
3. (Waldschmidt 2014)

4. Do the Work and Play

1. (Witherspoon 2002)
2. (DeBenedet 2018)
3. (Otter.ai 2022)
4. (Nuance 2022)

5. Establishing WHY

1. (Thurman 1980)
2. (Sinek 2009)
3. (Sinek 2017)
4. (Sinek 2017)

6. Disconnection and Creativity

1. (Picasso n.d.)
2. (Gaspirtz 2016)

8. Zigging and Zagging

1. (Oh and Pompeo 2005)
2. (GoodNotes 2022)
3. (Sreechinth 2016)
4. (Parton 2013)

9. The Beauty of Finished

1. (Laozi 1990)
2. (King 2002)

10. A Sassy Mindset

1. (Martin 2004)
2. (Augustine 1986)

about the author

Cassie Newell is a certified book coach, author, podcaster, and graphic designer. Cassie coaches writers through her Sassy Writing Coach platform with online courses and coaching services.

Cassie is originally from Tennessee where she gained the nick name Sassy Cassie from an early age. She is a nomad from various states and countries, currently calling home to sunny Florida with her family where she cheers on her favorite hockey team, Tampa Bay Lightning.

To get more information check out:
https://www.sassywritingcoach.com

acknowledgments

A special thank you to my partner in podcasting and coaching crimes, Shane Millar. This book is a book of my heart, and it felt raw at times. Shane, ever the writing coach, challenged and cheered me all the way, while trudging through the first disastrous page reads.

Thank you to the fabulous editor, Aime Sund of Red Leaf Word Services. You said, "bring on the Sassy!" and it freed me! Now my words are all dressed up and ready to help others. This book improved and now shines because of your thoughts, encouragement, and expertise.

Amy Harrington, my writing coach for this book, thank you for your guidance and support to say—Yes, yes, yes—I *had* to write this book. Your guidance provided the framework that is growing; the adventure is just starting.

A shout out to the Queen of Rebels, Sacha Black, a mentor and a friend, who encouraged me to write non-fiction and spread my wings while leaning into who I am now and still growing into.

To my clients, the writing tribes, and the communities I haunt, thank you for your trust and your ongoing support. You all inspire me to continue, and this means more than you know.

Last, but always first, is my husband, Butch. You are the best and thank you for always supporting me and being my first reader. The dream is not possible without you. I wish all writers had the type of support I have. Butch, you are one in a billion and I'm so blessed to have you in my life. Remember who kissed who first.

other titles by cassie newell

NonFiction

Writer Fuel

Spark & Start Your Story *(creative writing journal)*

Develop Your Idea Into A Story Premise (workbook)

For more details you can find more here:

www.sassywritingcoach.com

Fiction

YA Fantasy Novels Under C. M. Newell

For more details you can find more here:

www.authorcmnewell.com